2002 Barnes & Noble Books

ISBN 0 7607 2888 7

10 9 8 7 6 5 4 3 2

RANDOM HOUSE CHILDREN'S BOOKS
61–63 Uxbridge Road, London W5 5SA
A division of The Random House Group Ltd

RANDOM HOUSE AUSTRALIA (PTY) LTD
20 Alfred Street, Milsons Point, Sydney,
New South Wales 2061, Australia

RANDOM HOUSE NEW ZEALAND LTD
18 Poland Road, Glenfield, Auckland 10, New Zealand

RANDOM HOUSE (PTY) LTD
Endulini, 5A Jubilee Road, Parktown 2193, South Africa

THE RANDOM HOUSE GROUP Limited Reg. No. 954009

A CIP catalogue record for this book is available from the British Library.

Printed in Singapore

Little Bear's ABC

JANE HISSEY

BARNES
&NOBLE
BOOKS

a b c d e f g h i j k l m

A a

A is for animals. All the animals are asleep
except Little Bear.

Bb

B is for box. Bramwell Brown has a big box
of buttons.

a b c d e f g h i j k l m

C c

C is for cake. Bramwell is cutting a piece for Camel.

n o p q r s t u v w x y z

Dd

D is for doll. She is wearing a blue dress and hat.

a b c d **e f** g h i j k l m

E is for egg. Be extra careful, Little Bear.
Please don't drop it.

Ff

F is for food. This picnic food looks fun to eat.

Gg

G is for game. The toys are playing a game of hide-and-seek. Can you find them?

Hh

H is for holding on. Hold on tight, Little Bear,
Hoot is flying high.

a b c d e f g h i j k l m

I i

I is for inside. Little Bear is inside his sleeping bag.

J j

J is for jelly. Don't jump in Ruff's birthday jelly, Little Bear.

a b c d e f g h i j **k** l m

K is for kangaroo. She is kicking a big red ball.

L l

L is for leaf. Don't let go, Little Bear.

Mm

M is for marbles. How many marbles has Cat found?

Nn

N is for nest. Hoot's new nest is a nice woolly hat.

a b c d e f g h i j k l m

O o

O is for on. Old Bear is sitting on top of a basket watching Little Bear.

P p

P is for present. This one is wrapped in pretty paper.

Q q

Q is for quiet please. Old Bear is sleeping under his quilt.

R r

R is for run. Rabbit is running in a race.

S s

S is for sand, small stones and a spade.

Tt

T is for tent. These two friends are camping
in the garden.

U u

U is for upside down. There are four bricks under Little Bear.

Vv

V is for vase. That's not a very good hiding place, Rabbit!

a b c d e f g h i j k l m

W is for wool. I wonder what Bramwell Brown is knitting?

X x

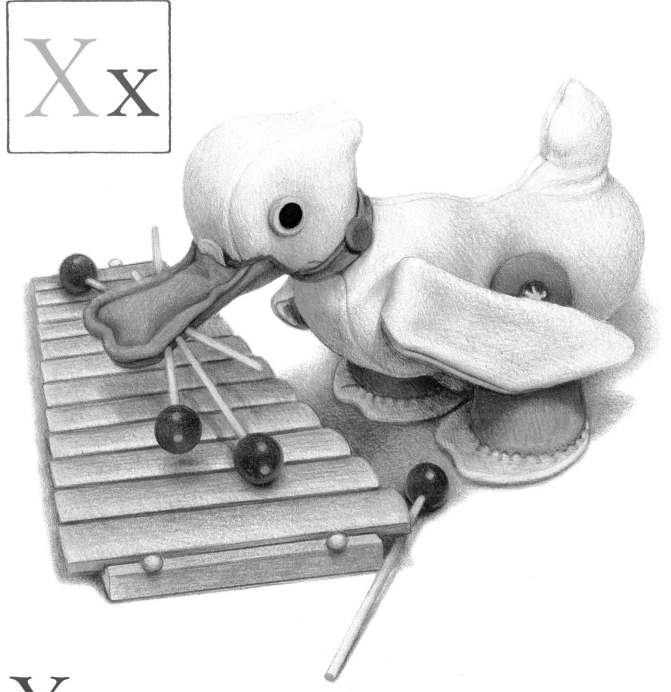

X is for xylophone. Duck is playing some music.

a b c d e f g h i j k l m

Yy

Y is for yellow. Can you see two yellow ducks?

Z z

Z is for Zebra. What is she pulling in her little red cart?

Some letters make new sounds
when they are side by side.

Sh

Th

ch

Ch

th

sh

Ch

Ch is for choose. Little Bear has chosen a chalk to write with.

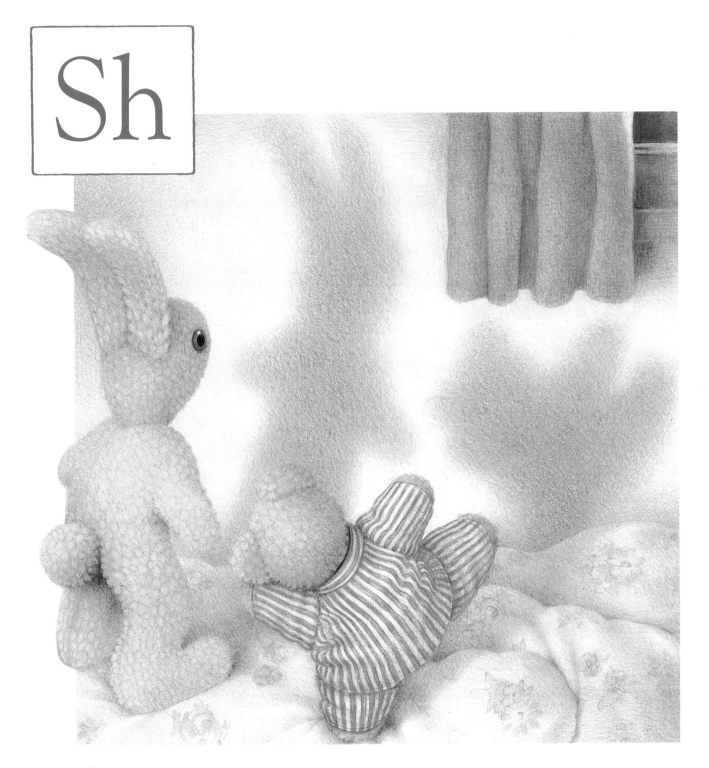

Sh

Sh is for shadows. Little Bear is showing Rabbit
his shadow picture on the wall.

Th

Th is for things. What letters do the things on the shelves begin with?

Little Bear's
123

1 2 3 4 5 6 7 8 9 10

1
one

1 sock

1 2 3 4 5 6 7 8 9 10

There is one candle on Ruff's birthday cake.

1 2 3 4 5 6 7 8 9 10

2
two

2 buckets

1 2 3 4 5 6 7 8 9 10

Rabbit has two skis on his feet.

1 2 3 4 5 6 7 8 9 10

3
three

3 bears

1 2 3 4 5 6 7 8 9 10

Here are three naughty toys jumping on the bed.

4
four

4 boots

1 2 3 **4** 5 6 7 8 9 10

Where is Dog hiding his four rubber bones?

5
five

5 biscuits

1 2 3 4 **5** 6 7 8 9 10

Here are five bears in a basket.

1 2 3 4 5 6 7 8 9 10

6
six

6 candles

1 2 3 4 5 6 7 8 9 10

Little Bear and Ruff have six bouncy balls.

1 2 3 4 5 6 **7** 8 9 10

7
seven

7 books

1 2 3 4 5 6 7 8 9 10

Can you see seven hats?

1 2 3 4 5 6 7 8 9 10

8
eight

8 paintbrushes

1 2 3 4 5 6 7 8 9 10

Old Bear is catching eight pieces of pink paper.

1 2 3 4 5 6 7 8 **9** 10

9
nine

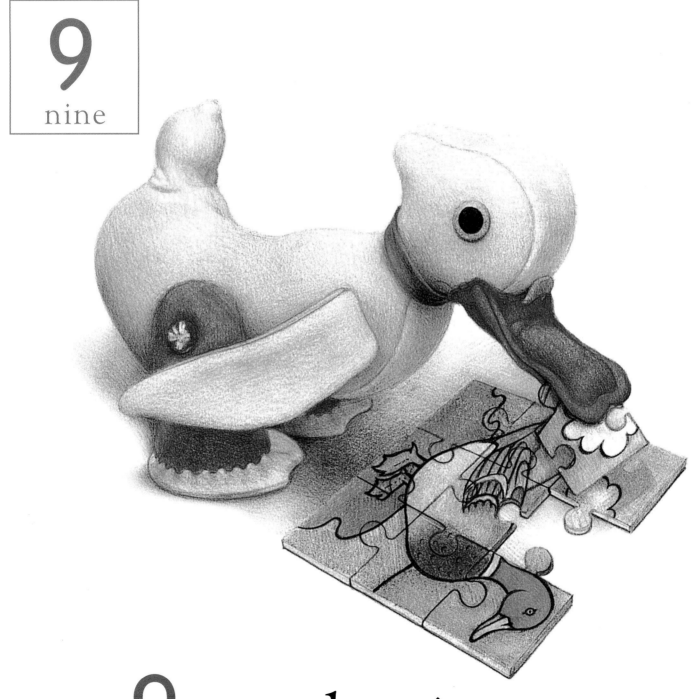

9 puzzle pieces

1 2 3 4 5 6 7 8 9 10

There are nine blue bubbles floating in the air.

1 2 3 4 5 6 7 8 9 10

10
ten

10 sticks

1 2 3 4 5 6 7 8 9 **10**

Ruff is driving his train over ten coloured pencils.

The toys are playing hide-and-seek. Let's help
Old Bear count to ten.

6 six 7 seven 8 eight 9 nine 10 ten

Can you guess how many friends he will find?

1 one 2 two 3 three 4 four 5 five

How many different things can you count?

Toys, hats, flags, bricks, bears, noses and ears!

1 4 d u t 10 h c 5 2 b z f